52
THINGS TO DO
— WITH A —
BEER

52 THINGS TO DO WITH A BEER

JAMES STEEN

Michael O'Mara Books Limited

First published in Great Britain in 2026 by
Michael O'Mara Books Limited
9 Lion Yard
Tremadoc Road
London SW4 7NQ

EU representative:
Authorised Rep Compliance Ltd
Ground Floor, 71 Baggot Street Lower
Dublin D02 P593
Ireland

Copyright © Michael O'Mara Books Limited 2026

All rights reserved. You may not copy, store, distribute, transmit, reproduce or otherwise make available this publication (or any part of it) in any form, or by any means (electronic, digital, optical, mechanical, photocopying, recording, machine readable, text/data mining or otherwise), without the prior written permission of the publisher. Any person who does any unauthorized act in relation to this publication may be liable to criminal prosecution and civil claims for damages.

A CIP catalogue record for this book is available from the British Library.

This product is made of material from well-managed, FSC®-certified forests and other controlled sources. The manufacturing processes conform to the environmental regulations of the country of origin.

For further information see www.mombooks.com/about/sustainability-climate-focus
Report any safety issues to product.safety@mombooks.com and see
www.mombooks.com/contact/product-safety

The author and the publisher disclaim any liability for any injury, accidents or loss that may occur as a result of information or instructions given in this book.

UK edition:
ISBN: 978-1-78929-880-2 in hardback print format

US edition:
ISBN: 978-1-78929-915-1 in hardback print format

1 2 3 4 5 6 7 8 9 10

Cover design by Natasha Le Coultre
Designed and typeset by Natasha Le Coultre and Claire Cater
Illustrations from www.shutterstock.com
Printed and bound in China

www.mombooks.com

CONTENTS

	Before You Pour …	8
1	Drink a Beer	10
2	Recipe: Guinness and Brown-Bread Ice Cream	13
3	George Washington's Small Beer	16
4	Compile a Beer Playlist	18
5	Split the G	20
6	Guinness World Records	22
7	Cocktail: Butterbeer, Buttered Beer, Buttered Ale	24
8	Bucket List Beer Trips	26
9	Cocktail: Dublin Slammer	28
10	Recipe: Beer Batter	30
11	Cocktail: Guinness Punch	32
12	Recipe: Moules Marinière	34
13	Books, Authors and Beer	36
14	Recipe: Easy Guinness Glaze for Ham	38
15	Cocktail: Guinness Martini	40
16	Beer Festivals	42

17	Recipe: Pale Ale Pickles	45
18	Host a Guinness Tasting Night	48
19	Recipe: Beer Can Chicken	50
20	A Beer Trap for Garden Pests	52
21	Cocktail: Guinness Black Russian	54
22	Recipe: Bierkäsesuppe	56
23	Beer (Bottle) Glasses	58
24	Beer Bath	60
25	White House Beers	62
26	Musical Interlude – *Roll Out the Barrel*	64
27	Recipe: Carbonnade à la Flamande	68
28	Cheers to Beer! Raise a Glass to Beer Day	70
29	Beer Face Mask	73
30	Recipe: Welsh Rarebit aka Grilled Cheese	75
31	Go Green	77
32	Recipe: IPA Hot Sauce	79
33	Hangover Cure: Michelada (Mexican Bloody Mary)	81
34	Recipe: Chocolate, Orange and Walnut Stout Cake	83
35	Beero	86

36	Brew Your Own	88
37	Recipe: Beef Brisket in Guinness and Prune Juice	91
38	Bottle Cap Clock	94
39	The Beer Bottle Garden Game (with Lots of Names)	96
40	Movie Drinking Games	98
41	Brewlette	100
42	Cocktail: Black Velvet	103
43	How Green is Your Garden?	106
44	Recipe: Beer Blinis	108
45	Guinness Selfie	110
46	Recipe: Beer Syrup	112
47	Paint with Beer	114
48	Beer Salt	118
49	Beer-rings	120
50	Chocolate Stout and Ice Cream Float	122
51	… And Float with Beer	124
52	Recipe: Beer Granita	126
	About the Author / Acknowledgements	128

BEFORE YOU POUR ...

The great philosopher Plato declared: 'Whoever invented beer is a wise man.' How right he was. Beer has been a gift from the gods for at least five thousand – perhaps eight thousand – years. There is evidence of beer being brewed in the ancient regions of Samaria and Mesopotamia. Although then it was a thick, porridge-like affair sweetened with honey, not quite the pleasure that we know today.

Over the millennia, beer has been there, making us happy at feasts and banquets, parties and gatherings. How many glasses brimming with beer have been raised to this or to that?

Here, a glass is raised to beer itself. Within these pages you will find fifty-two salutes to the great beverage made from hops, yeast, malted barley and water, with the addition of honey back in Plato's day. That's one entry for each week of the year, and each one pays tribute to that ancient symbol of unity, friendship and community.

The entries include recipes for dishes made with beer, from comforting snacks of Cheddar Beer Rarebit and German beer-cheese soup, to a hearty beef brisket in Guinness and prune sauce. If you are a baker, try the Chocolate, Orange and Walnut Stout Cake or Guinness and Brown-Bread Ice Cream (and drizzle it with the Beer Syrup). Fancy a cocktail? If so, rustle up a Guinness Black Russian or Black Velvet, or on a summer's day make Guinness Punch. Flit around the world within these pages to read about people and places, literature and games – all with an interesting beer connection.

We are not only here for drinking beer. Discover great beer hacks for cleaning, bathing and gardening. Meanwhile, the barrel is rolled out with a bit of music and games to play with empty beer bottles and beer caps. Always drink responsibly, but if you do overindulge, try a Michelada (Mexican Bloody Mary), an effective hair of the dog. Just like the best bar, this book is a dip in, dip out sort of place, where a glass is always raised to … beer. Cheers! Bottoms up! Sláinte! And good health!

Pour, sip, enjoy. Simply drink a beer and enjoy it. And as you do so, consider any part of the process that has brought this joy into your life.

It is a process that begins with harvesting the barley in the farmer's field. The barley then undergoes malting, which in itself requires various steps. First it is given moisture (the first stage is 'steeping'), then there is germination when rootlets appear. This is followed by kilning. At the start, the grain tastes like grass seed; by the end of the malting process it tastes a bit like those malt drinks, Ovaltine or Horlicks. (Maltesers are also made from malt extract.)

The grain is milled and then mashed with water so that it resembles a giant porridge (and the ratio of water to grain is similar to porridge). This is then separated. The enzymes that were produced in the malting process can now work on the starch, producing soluble sugars. The resulting sweet nutritious solution called 'wort' is then separated and boiled with hops, and then fermented, when yeast is added.

Lager, meanwhile, requires its own species of yeast, which operates at lower temperatures. Compared with other beer, it takes longer to ferment and achieve the taste profiles. Extra time in the barrel means extra storage time. Hence, the German word *Lager* means 'store' in English.

Recipe

GUINNESS AND BROWN-BREAD ICE CREAM

 Makes 2 medium-sized tubs, each about 500ml/17 fl oz

- 300ml/2 cups double/heavy cream
- 200ml/7 fl oz whole milk
- 1 tsp grated nutmeg
- 4 medium egg yolks
- 90g/½ cup caster/baker's sugar
- 50g/1½ oz muscovado/dark brown sugar
- 100ml/½ cup Guinness or other stout
- 150g/1½ cups good-quality brown bread (Irish soda bread, perhaps)
- 50g/1½ oz hazelnuts
- icing/powdered sugar, to dust the nuts and crumbled bread

1. Pour the cream and milk into a medium saucepan, add the nutmeg and heat gently, stirring occasionally, and bring to the boil.

2. Meanwhile, in a large heat-proof bowl, whisk the egg yolks with the caster/baker's sugar.

3. Pour the hot infused cream into the egg mixture, whisking while you go. Return the cream-egg mixture to the saucepan and place over a low heat, stirring with a spatula until the crème anglaise (custard) thinly coats the back of the spatula. Do not bring it to the boil as it will scramble.

4. Return the mixture to the bowl and leave it to cool to room temperature – stir occasionally to help it cool. Cover the mixture and refrigerate for at least 4 hours.

5. In a saucepan, bring the stout and muscovado/dark brown sugar to the boil and let it reduce by about half. Leave it to cool to room temperature. Once cooled, combine it with the cooled crème anglaise.

Meanwhile, to toast and caramelize the nuts and crumbled bread, preheat the oven to 180°C/350°F.

 Coarsely chop the nuts and spread them on a shallow lined baking tray and sprinkle with icing sugar. Sprinkle a little water over the nuts and sugar. Bake for about 8 minutes, tossing them occasionally so they don't burn and then transfer to a plate. Crumble the bread – not too small, so as to keep some texture. Now spread the bread over the tray, sprinkle with sugar and a little water, and place in the oven to toast. Turn over the crumbs to prevent burning.

 Now combine the chilled crème anglaise with the reduced stout and stir in the nuts and toasted bread. Transfer the mixture to an ice cream machine and churn. Put in a container and freeze until required.

Are you an American history buff? If so, you may wish to make George Washington's 'small beer'.

Relatively low in alcohol as it is the weakest brew, small beer was enjoyed long before Washington's time. The Tudors knew it was safer than water, and they drank it from breakfast onwards.

Washington, a true connoisseur, wrote the recipe in his notebook of 1757, when he was twenty-five years old and a young colonel during the French and Indian War (and thirty-two years before he became the first president of the United States).

For his thirty-gallon brew, bran hops were boiled for three hours. Next, three gallons of molasses were added to the boiling brans while 'scalding hot'. The mixture was left to stand until blood-warm, and then yeast was added. Washington noted that 'if the weather is very cold, cover it [the beer] over with a blank[et]'. It was left to work in the cooler for twenty-four hours and then transferred to a cask and bottled the week it was brewed.

COMPILE A BEER PLAYLIST

Beer, like music, has the power to transport us. It is not just a drink but a mood, a ritual, a celebration. So why not pair your brew with a playlist?

Whether you're drinking solo after work, hosting a barbecue or in a bar with your friends, elevate the experience by accompanying it with the right song.

Check out 'Beer for My Horses' by Toby Keith and Willie Nelson (it's a country anthem about fighting injustice and celebrating winnings, straight from the Wild West). Actually, an extremely long beer playlist could be compiled entirely from Country and Western because most songs in this genre mention the drink, and that includes Johnny Cash's 'I Hardly Ever Sing Beer Drinking Songs'.

For something louder, 'Beer Drinkers & Hell Raisers' by ZZ Top offers a foot-stomping ode to the fast life. Keep things going with George Thorogood's 'One Bourbon, One Scotch, One Beer', a bluesy slow-burner that's pure barroom storytelling. You might also like to include 'Roll Out the Barrel' (aka 'The Beer Barrel Polka'): see page 64.

Someone, somewhere, sometime started this craze. Who was it? No one knows. When and where did it originate?

No one knows, though it seems most likely a modern creation rather than an ancient tradition.

The challenge is easy – you drink sufficient first gulps of the beer, so that the top of the foam cuts across the 'G' of the Guinness sign printed on the pint glass. In fact, when it comes to the challenge, Guinness aficionados are, erm, split.

Those up for the challenge believe that the drink is best enjoyed at the beginning when it is gulped – five or six successive swigs in one. This, they say, allows the drinker to fully appreciate the creamy texture and taste, as well as benefitting from a refreshing hit. Those against the challenge say that it is simply too much to drink in one go, and that really it is better to split the harp which sits above 'Guinness' on the glass and so requires only a couple of big gulps.

6
GUINNESS
WORLD RECORDS

The Guinness World Records were created in the 1950s, after a shooting party.

Sir Hugh Beaver, managing director of the Guinness Brewery, had a disagreement: which is the fastest game bird in Europe?

Beaver said it was the golden plover. His shooting companion insisted it was the red grouse. (They were both wrong – the fastest game bird is the red-breasted merganser.) Anyway, it sparked the idea for a book of facts – what later became known as the *Guinness Book of World Records*.

Beery feats which hold Guinness World Records include the fastest pint of Guinness drunk (0.45 seconds) and 'high-speed gulping' (three pints in 31 seconds). Meanwhile, superhuman John Evans balanced 237 pints on his head.

In the summer of 2014, regulars excitedly gathered at The Fleece Countryside Inn in Ripponden, West Yorkshire, to witness the unveiling of the world's largest-ever glass of beer. Created by British company Stod Fold Brewing Company, the glass held 2,082l (3,664 pts) of Stod Fold Gold Ale. The glass was 2.23m (7 ft 4 in) tall and 1.12m (3 ft 8 in) in diameter.

Cocktail

BUTTERBEER, BUTTERED BEER, BUTTERED ALE

Butterbeer features frequently in *Harry Potter*. Drunk while it is still foaming, it is 'a popular wizarding beverage', and while low in alcohol, it leaves the little house elves drunk.

The butterbeer that we know from Potter is 'slightly less sickly than butterscotch'.

Meanwhile, the Tudors enjoyed buttered beer (or buttered ale), which had plenty of alcohol. A note of caution … Samuel Pepys, in his diaries of April 1665, spoke of 'my cold continuing and my stomach sick with the buttered ale that I did drink the last night in bed, which did lie upon me till I did this morning vomitt it up'. It is an interesting alternative to mulled/spiced wine or eggnog at Christmas. Back in 1594, Thomas Dawson gave a recipe in his cookery book *The Good Huswife's Handmaide for the Kitchin*. Here's a modern-day version …

 Serves 6

- 3 pints/60 fl oz good ale
- 5 egg yolks, whisked
- 100g/3½ oz caster/baker's sugar (I've reduced Dawson's sugar quantity)
- 6 cloves
- ½ tsp ground cinnamon
- ½ tsp ground ginger
- 30g/1 oz cold butter cubes

 In a large saucepan, gently heat 3 pints/60 fl oz of good ale with 5 whisked egg yolks; 100g/3½ oz caster sugar (have reduced the Dawson's sugar quantity); 6 cloves; ½ tsp ground cinnamon; ½ tsp ground ginger. Just before serving, whisk in 30g/1 oz cold butter cubes.

 Serve warm, like mulled/spiced wine, or refrigerate and serve chilled. The result is sweet, creamy and malty. Who knew the Tudors gave us Horlicks?!

8 BUCKET LIST BEER TRIPS

Pack your tankard and take a trip ...

Go to Colorado, where they produce more beer than any other state (14.2 million barrels in the first three quarters of 2024). If you're into craft beer, California tops craft beer production overall (over 3.55 million barrels in 2022).

Or visit the oldest brewery in the United States. Established in 1829, family-owned Yuengling is based in Pennsylvania and is one of the biggest craft breweries by volume.

The ever-cheerful city of Portland, Oregon, has the greatest number of breweries of any city in the world. It has more than seventy breweries within city limits (hence its nickname, Beervana).

You might like to visit the Bingley Arms in Bardsey, West Yorkshire, as it is widely considered the oldest pub in Britain, said to date back to AD 953. While the British pub with the longest name is in Staylbridge, Greater Manchester – The Old Thirteenth Cheshire Astley Volunteer Rifleman Corps Inn (try saying that after a few pints). Check out a few of Britain's largest pubs: the Moon Under Water on Deansgate, Manchester; BrewDog Waterloo (a staggering distance from the station); and Royal Victoria Pavilion in Ramsgate, Kent.

Cocktail

DUBLIN SLAMMER

Also known as an Irish Slammer or Dublin Drop.

This is the Irish cousin of two drinks which originated in the United States: Boilermaker (in which a shot of Bourbon is dropped into a glass of beer) and Jägerbomb (a shot of the German herby digestif, Jägermeister, is dropped into a glass of Red Bull). Meanwhile, a Skittle Bomb is a shot of Cointreau dropped into Red Bull, and a Sake Bomb is sake dropped into beer, preferably Japanese.

 **Serves 1**

- 1 can Guinness (or your preferred stout)
- Irish whiskey
- Irish cream liqueur (such as Baileys Irish Cream)

 Half fill a pint glass with Guinness (or your preferred stout). Half fill a shot glass with Irish cream liqueur, such as Bailey's Irish Cream. Top up the glass with Irish whiskey.

 Drop the shot glass into the Guinness. Drink to Ireland and then slam your glass on the counter.

⇛⇛⇛ *Recipe* ⇚⇚⇚
BEER BATTER

A light batter perfect for coating fish and sliced vegetables before deep frying them in hot oil until crispy and golden.

 Makes about 300ml/10 fl oz

- 2 medium eggs
- 25g/1 oz unsalted butter, melted

- 100g/3½ oz plain/all-purpose flour
- 100ml/3½ fl oz cold beer or lager

 In a large bowl, whisk the eggs with the melted butter until fully incorporated and foamy. Whisk in the flour, little by little. Pour in the beer and gently stir.

 Lay the ingredients – be it fish or sliced vegetables – into the batter until fully coated.

 Heat vegetable oil in a deep-sided saucepan or a deep fryer, and fry at 170°C/340°F. To test if the oil is hot enough, simply spoon a little batter into the oil and if it sizzles then you're good to go.

 Transfer the batter-coated ingredients to the hot oil, and cook in batches so as not to overcrowd the pan. Fry until crisp and golden.

For party snacks, try courgette (zucchini) fritters: slice the vegetable into long strips, coat in batter, deep fry, season with sea-salt flakes and squeeze with lemon juice. Or cut fillets of fish (such as cod, haddock or pollock) into five chunks and deep fry them in this batter. Squeeze with lemon, season and serve with tartar sauce.

Cocktail

GUINNESS PUNCH

**'I'm coming over to yours to make a Jamaican feast.'
This was back in 2019, and on the other end of the line
was Levi Roots, Britain's best-loved Rasta cook.**

The following day he arrived at my home to do as he'd promised. He played Bob Marley at full blast as he rustled up lots of dishes, which included juicy jerk chicken, patties and a huge pan of rice and peas. Then my family and I sat down with Levi and remained at the table for hours.

The Jamaican-born author of the *Reggae Reggae Cookbook* and *Caribbean Food Made Easy* also made Guinness Punch.

It's a traditional Irish-Caribbean delight and certainly put a sweet swing into our little party.

 Serves 6

- 3 pints/60 fl oz Guinness
- 400g/14 oz sweetened condensed milk
- 100g/3½ oz evaporated milk
- 2 pinches of ground nutmeg and a pinch of cinnamon (Note: Levi also added a teaspoon of vanilla essence, but that's optional.)

 Pour the Guinness into a large jug. Add the condensed milk, evaporated milk, nutmeg and cinnamon. Add vanilla essence, if using.

 Stir well and, if you wish, refrigerate. Fill 6 large glasses with ice cubes and divide the Guinness punch between the glasses. Serve.

P.S. Levi's kindness was not forgotten, of course. I bought him a fat turkey to roast on Christmas Day and delivered it to him at his home in Brixton, the renowned rasta chill-spot of south-west London.

Recipe

MOULES MARINIÈRE

Mussels, sailor style.

Often this dish is made with wine, but that can be replaced with your beer (or cider) of choice, though you might opt for French or Belgian. It's quick: about 10 minutes to prep the mussels, about 10 minutes to cook.

 Serves 4

- 1.8kg/4 lb fresh mussels
- 50g/2 tbsp unsalted butter
- 3 bay leaves
- 4 thyme sprigs
- 1 medium white onion, finely diced

- 3 sprigs flat-leaf parsley, coarsely chopped
- 200ml/7 fl oz beer
- 3 tbsp double/heavy cream (optional)

First, prep the mussels. Discard any mussels which are not tightly closed before you begin to cook. Wash the mussels in a large bowl under cold running water. Mussels that float at this stage are not fresh, so discard them. Remove any beards and loose barnacles, but don't scrub the shells (as it will colour the finished dish). Drain.

In a large saucepan over a high heat, melt the butter. Add the onion, bay leaves and thyme, stir and then pour in the beer. Bring to the boil, add the mussels and cover with a lid to keep in the steam.

Let the mussels cook in that steam for about 5 minutes, until all the shells have opened. Throw in the chopped parsley and, if using, add the cream, replace the lid and gently shake the pan. Serve with sliced baguette and beer.

What a joy it is to read a book with a beer at your side! Which you might be doing right now.

Bury your nose in the pages, and then in a glass, and consider how our best authors and playwrights have long used beer, ale and porter to bring characters to life and for symbolism in their narrative.

Beer is there in Shakespeare's plays and Chaucer's *Canterbury Tales*. While through his masterpieces, Charles Dickens incorporates beer, pubs and breweries to fully capture Victorian England. In *The Pickwick Papers*, London's The George and Vulture is almost its own character – Dickens drank there often and especially enjoyed a 'half and half' (an equal mix of ale and porter). His wine cellar at home, Gad's Hill in Kent, featured a 50-gallon cask of ale. That's 400 pints. Hardly a bleak house.

F. Scott Fitzgerald finds space for beer in novels such as *The Great Gatsby*. He and his wife Zelda drank Bass Pale Ale when they lived in New York. When in Germany in 1925, Fitzgerald adored the 'Pilsen and Munich beer of fine quality'. Well-known for his unquenchable thirst, he is quoted as saying: 'There is less than there was when I got here.'

Recipe

EASY GUINNESS GLAZE FOR HAM

A delicious glaze for cooked hams that is spicy, sweet and rich. The Guinness can be replaced by another stout, such as Murphy's or Beamish.

 Makes enough for a 5kg/11 lb ham

- 2 tbsp English mustard
- 100ml/3½ fl oz Guinness, Murphy's or Beamish
- 4 tbsp runny honey
- 2 tbsp muscovado/dark brown sugar
- 1 orange, juice only

- ½ tsp black peppercorns, finely ground
- 1 tsp cloves, finely ground

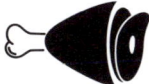

 Combine all the ingredients in a bowl – but using only half of the Guinness.

 Transfer the mixture to a sauté pan/skillet and bring to a boil over a medium heat, and let it reduce by half. Now, keeping the pan on the heat, pour in the remaining Guinness little by little, and continue to cook until the glaze is thick and syrupy.

 Using a pastry brush, cover the top and sides of the ham with the hot glaze. Leave to cool, and then carve and serve with potato salad, mustard, pickles and glasses of stout.

Cocktail

GUINNESS MARTINI

If James Bond ever found himself in Dublin on a rainy night, this might be his drink of choice.

The Guinness Martini is where the depth of a classic stout collides with the sharp elegance of a cocktail. It's beer with a twist. Or it's an espresso martini with a shot of Guinness.

The standard recipe usually calls for Guinness (or Guinness reduction), vodka and coffee liqueur. Some versions use cold espresso, while Irish cream gives a velvety finish. Decorate with a coffee bean. Here's proof that beer doesn't always have to come in a pint glass – sometimes it deserves a stem. Stir one up, cue something moody on the playlist (see page 18) and raise a toast to the beer cocktail you didn't know you needed.

 Serves 1

- 25ml/1 fl oz vodka
- 50ml/2 fl oz Guinness (original stout, draught preferred)
- 25ml/1 fl oz Kahlúa (or other coffee liqueur)
- 1 dessertspoon Irish cream liqueur (for extra creaminess)

 Pour all the ingredients into a jug of ice, stir and strain into a martini glass. Decorate with a coffee bean.

There are thousands of beer festivals every year, big and small. Here are a few of the best ...

Germany:
Brush up on your polka and your German (*Bierkrug* means beer mug) and move to Munich for three weeks in the autumn ... *Oktoberfest* is the world's largest beer festival. The average annual beer consumption at *Oktoberfest* – swigged to the music of puffing accordions – is 7 million litres (about 12 million pints and, for Americans, 14 million beers). *Prost!*

United States:
The *Great American Beer Festival* in Denver, Colorado, is the largest ticketed beer event in the United States. Meanwhile the *Oregon Brewers Festival* in Portland, Oregon, is a massive outdoor party on the city's waterfront.

The Island of Ireland:
Dublin Beer Festival was launched in 2011 and celebrates 200 beers from Ireland and across the world. *The Hagstravangza* at the White Hag Brewery in Co. Sligo, on

Ireland's Wild Atlantic Way, is a summer celebration of Irish craft beer with live bands too. What a craic! *Portrush Beer Fest* in the seaside town of Portrush (population: 6,000) in Co. Antrim, Northern Ireland, comes alive for this two-day event.

United Kingdom:

The *Great British Beer Festival*, held every August, is the nation's biggest beer festival, with 900 beers, ciders and perries. It is organized by the Campaign for Real Ale (CAMRA).

Canada:

Established in 1969, *Kitchener-Waterloo Beer Festival* in Ontario is the world's second-largest Bavarian beer fest. *Prost* again!

Recipe

PALE ALE PICKLES

Create your own easy-peasy pale ale pickled cucumbers.

Great with a burger or on salads. Chop them and add them – with chopped capers – to mayonnaise to make tartar sauce. Or simply enjoy them with a beer while reciting the tongue-twister about Peter Piper picking that peck of pickled peppers.

Makes 3 medium-sized jars

- 350ml/12 fl oz pale ale (1 bottle)
- 300ml/10 fl oz white wine vinegar
- 60ml/2 fl oz water
- 50g/⅓ cup caster/baker's sugar
- 2 pinches of sea-salt flakes
- a dozen peppercorns
- 3 dill sprigs
- 450g/1lb small unwaxed cucumbers
- option for spicy pickles: add sliced chilli to the pickle liquor

 Pour the beer, vinegar and water into a large saucepan. Add the sugar, salt and peppercorns. Place the pan on a high heat and boil for 30 seconds, or until the sugar has dissolved.

 Remove the pan from the heat, add the dill sprigs to the pan and leave to cool to room temperature.

Meanwhile, wash the cucumbers and quarter them lengthways and remove the seeds.

 Pack the cucumber in a 1L Kilner jar (or Mason jar). Pour in the pickle liquor until the cucumbers are immersed (push them down a little, if necessary).

 Seal the jar and refrigerate. The pickled cucumbers will be ready to eat in a week, and will keep for up to one month in the fridge before losing their texture.

18
HOST A
GUINNESS
TASTING NIGHT

There is more than one Guinness. In fact, there's a whole family of bold, complex brews waiting to be explored.

Host a fun and tasty Guinness tasting night to surprise your friends. The line-up could feature: Guinness Draught; Guinness 0.0 (non-alcoholic); Guinness Foreign Extra Stout; Guinness Cold Brew Coffee Beer; Guinness West Indies Porter; Guinness Original; and Guinness Blonde (a collaboration between Guinness and Pennsylvania brewery Latrobe).

Add a competitive twist by turning it into a blindfolded guessing game – Guess the Guinness – and see who really knows their stouts (this is perfect for that one irritating friend who claims constantly to be a Guinness expert). Or keep it relaxed with printed tasting notes and a taster's wheel to help guests pick out aromas and profiles like roasted barley, caramel, coffee or citrus.

Oops! Almost forgot the food! Complement your beers with mature cheddars, oysters or Guinness chocolates, or even a Guinness chocolate cake (see page 83).

Recipe

BEER CAN CHICKEN

This is fun – and delicious – on a summer's day. The beer steams in the heat of the barbecue. Result: seriously succulent crispy-skinned chicken.

 Serves 5–6

- 1 chicken (about 1.8kg/4 lb)
- 1 can of beer (440ml/ 15 fl oz)
- 2 rosemary sprigs
- extra virgin olive oil
- 1 tbsp brown sugar

 First, consider the space in the barbecue – once the chicken is in and standing upright, the lid will need to be closed. Light the BBQ and let it heat up.

 Use a can opener to open the beer can. Pour half the beer into a glass (this can be drunk).

 Season inside the chicken's main cavity with salt and pepper. Push the rosemary sprigs into the main cavity. Sit the chicken on top of the half-filled beer can, so that now the top of the can is in the chicken's main cavity. Mix the olive oil and sugar to form a paste and brush this over the chicken.

 Now stand the chicken-and-can upright in the hot barbie. Close the lid.

 Barbecue for about 1 hour 30 minutes. Test with a food probe: the chicken is cooked when the thickest part of the thigh is 75–80°C/165–175°F. Loosely cover the beer can chicken with foil and leave to rest for 20–30 minutes before serving.

Beer is a blessing for gardeners.

Sure, it's refreshing to relax and enjoy a chilled drink after a day of weeding beneath the hot summer sun. However, beer can also help rid the garden of pests.

Wasps and mosquitoes are said to be drawn to it, but slugs are especially attracted to the yeast in beer. In fact, they seem to like it more than lettuces, cabbages and carrots.

In 2019, Garden Organic conducted an experiment in an effort to establish just how much slugs love this drink. The charity found that over a four-day period, beer traps caught an average five slugs while those containers filled with lager caught six slugs. Cheap lager may have a higher yeast content – a deliriously intoxicating scent for the slimy menaces. It's not only friendly to the environment but also cost-effective, as a can of inexpensive lager is cheaper than nasty chemicals.

A beer trap is easy to make. Use a clean and recyclable container, such as a used yogurt pot, food can or takeaway carton, or even half a beer can. Bury the container, open side up, so that its rim is slightly above the soil line. Pour in the beer, which can be old and flat. When necessary, empty the container of dead slugs and replenish with beer.

Cocktail

GUINNESS BLACK RUSSIAN

Smooth but packs a punch. This is an insanely bold reinvention of the classic Black Russian, made deeper, darker and far more intriguing with the addition of stout and cola.

Consider it a long drink for a long night: rich, fizzy, layered. Perfect for when you're craving something between a cocktail and a pint, the Guinness Black Russian is complex and dangerously drinkable.

It is also well-balanced. Sweetness comes from the coffee

liqueur, the vodka gives it a clean bite, lime brings fresh zest and the fizz of the cola lifts everything. The Guinness pulls it all together; earthy, roasted and rich, it is the creamy, malty backbone of this cocktail.

 Serves 1

- ice
- 25ml/1 fl oz coffee liqueur
- 25ml/1 fl oz vodka
- 100ml/3½ fl oz cola

 Fill a tall glass (or highball) with ice. Pour in 25ml/1 fl oz coffee liqueur, 25ml/1 fl oz vodka and 100ml/3½ fl oz cola. Stir gently to combine.

 Then top with 100ml/3½ fl oz Guinness, letting the stout cascade through the glass. Garnish with a wedge of lime. No shaking, no fuss. Enjoy the fizzy, velvety experience.

Recipe
BIERKÄSESUPPE

Or Beer Cheese Soup. A hearty Germanic dish in which the cheese melts to become irresistibly ribboned and moreish.

 Serves 4

- 2 tbsp extra virgin olive oil
- 30g/2 tbsp unsalted butter
- 2 medium onions, finely chopped
- 1 celery stick, finely chopped
- 2 level tsp plain/all-purpose flour
- 600ml/20 fl oz Pilsner
- 200g/7 oz Gruyère or Emmental cheese, grated, plus a little extra to garnish

- 600ml/20 fl oz good quality chicken stock
- to season, sea-salt flakes and ground black pepper

 Heat the oil in a large saucepan (or casserole dish) over a low-medium heat. Add the butter, and when it foams, add the onion and celery, along with a few generous pinches of salt and black pepper. Sweat the vegetables for 6–8 minutes, stirring occasionally. Add the flour and continue to cook gently for about 5 minutes.

 Increase the heat to medium, pour in the beer, little by little, and let it come to the boil and then reduce by half. Pour in the chicken stock, bring it to the boil and then reduce the heat and let it simmer for 5 minutes.

 Remove the pan from the heat, add the grated cheese and stir until it has fully melted. Reheat if necessary and then taste to check the seasoning. Divide the soup between 4 bowls, sprinkle with the extra grated cheese, and serve.

23
BEER
(BOTTLE)
GLASSES

Heads-up: beer glasses are not easy to make.

You need to have excessive time to spare and a strong, almost unmanageable DIY streak. But for these glasses, you might need to do it yourself ... because no one else will unless you pay them.

The glasses are made from empty beer bottles, which should be carefully cut. The home version is achieved by soaking string in a flammable liquid and tying it around the beer bottle, below the neck. The string is set alight, which heats up the glass, and then the bottle is placed instantly in a tub of ice-cold water, creating thermal shock. The bottle should (!) snap at the string, where the glass is weakened. Finally, the rough edges are sanded until smooth, so you can drink from a glass without ending up looking like the Joker.

Top tip: Splash out on a specialized glass cutter in order to turn your best beer bottles into drinking glasses.

Beer bath? Yes, a beer bath. It's a medicinal thing and has been for centuries.

Spa Beerland is in the cellar of an old beer warehouse in Prague where 1,000-L oak tubs are filled with Czech Krušovice. Bathers submerge themselves and let the hop essential oils revitalize the skin.

According to Spa Beerland, the treatment 'stimulates metabolism, flushes harmful substances from the body, releases internal and external tension, fatigue and stress, and thus leads to perfect mental and physical relaxation. In the magical cellars from the Rudolphine era, you will be able to drink unlimited quantities of genuine Krušovice beer during the entire treatment.' More recent beer spas can be found in Belgium. A big plus ... the beer comes out of a tap so, as it flows, you can top up your glass.

The Vitamin B in brewer's yeast is another tonic for the skin – as well as the spirits. Hoppy, happy, feel-good therapy. If you don't happen to have enough to make your own beer bath, why not try a foot soak in beer? Simply fill a washing-up bowl with beer and a glass with beer, submerge your feet, drink and relax.

In 2011, President Obama was so inspired by America's home brewers that he decided to have a go himself and make beer at The White House.

He bought a home-brewing kit for the WH kitchen. Advice and tips followed, the brewing began.

Sam Kass – Obama's senior advisor for nutrition policy at the time – wrote about this pioneering adventure: 'To be honest, we were surprised that the beer turned out so well, since none of us had brewed beer before … As far as we know, The White House Honey Brown Ale is the first alcohol brewed or distilled on The White House grounds.' George Washington brewed beer at his Mount Vernon estate (see *George Washington's Small Beer*, page 16). Thomas Jefferson had vineyards at his Monticello plantation, though failed to produce wine.

Obama's first batch of White House Honey Brown Ale was followed by Honey Porter. Next came Honey Blonde. Why honey? The brews featured honey from beehives on the South Lawn. Installed by Michelle Obama, these may have been the first-ever beehives at The White House. 'The honey gives the beer a rich aroma and a nice finish, but it doesn't sweeten it,' said Kass. Recipes and kits for brewing these beers are online.

26 MUSICAL INTERLUDE

ROLL OUT THE BARREL

Enjoy a pint and sing along to 'Roll Out the Barrel'. A wartime classic, US Commander-in-Chief Ike Eisenhower partly credited the Allied victory to this morale-boosting song.

Go to any pub in London's East End, and the Cockneys will tell you that the song is theirs. Germans are also adamant the song originated in their country. Indeed, many nations (wrongly) claim it as their own.

The catchy melody was in fact written in 1927 by Czech composer Jaromír Vejvoda. He named it 'Modřanská Polka' after the Prague suburb of Modřany where the tune was first played. It was published in 1929 with lyrics by Vašek Zeman and entitled 'Skoda Lásky' (Unrequited Love).

In 1934, Shapiro Bernstein acquired the rights to the song. The English lyrics were added that same year, written by American lyricist Lew Brown (also famous for 'Don't Sit Under the Apple Tree') and the Russian-born composer Wladimir Timm. Entitled 'Beer Barrel Polka', the song heralded the end of America's Prohibition. In 1930s Germany, it was a hit for Will Glahé with the title 'Rosamunde'. Skipping forward to 1939, and at the outbreak of the World War II, it was released as 'Beer Barrel Polka' by The Andrews Sisters.

'WHEN ALL ELSE FAILS, THERE IS MUSIC. WHEN THAT FAILS YOU, THERE IS BEER.'

JAMES HAUENSTEIN

Recipe

CARBONNADE À LA FLAMANDE

A Flemish stew (the Dutch know it as *stoofvlees*) which is also enjoyed in north-east France.

Beef and vegetables are gently braised in beef stock and (you know what's coming) beer. Think *boeuf bourguignon* but made with Belgian beer rather than French wine.

 **Serves 4**

- 1.6kg/3½ lb beef shin pieces
- 1 tbsp plain/all-purpose flour
- 3 tbsp extra virgin olive oil
- 3 medium onions, finely chopped
- 2 medium carrots, coarsely chopped
- 6 garlic cloves, finely sliced
- 2 bay leaves
- 6 cloves
- 6 juniper berries (optional)
- 400ml/13½ fl oz beef stock
- 400ml/13½ fl oz Belgian dark beer

Preheat the oven to 170°C/340°F. Season the beef with salt and pepper, pressing the seasoning onto the beef. Dust with the flour.

Heat the oil in a large casserole over a low-medium heat, add the onions and carrots and bay, and gently sweat them for 5 minutes. Add the beef pieces, garlic, cloves and, if using, juniper berries. Season with salt and pepper.

Pour in the stock and beer, gently stir and bring to the boil, then cover with a lid and transfer to the oven. After 20 minutes, reduce the heat to 140°C/285°F and continue to cook for 2½ hours. Best served with Belgian fries or buttery, fluffy mashed potatoes.

28

CHEERS TO BEER!

Raise a Glass to
BEER DAY

As if you needed an excuse. Stock up, invite friends over and commemorate the day that celebrates beer. The international salute to the drink falls on the first Friday of every August. Meanwhile ...

United States

National Beer Day is celebrated on 7 April. This marks the day in 1933 when beer and wine could legally be sold. There was a bit of a kicker – the drinks were not allowed to have an alcohol content higher than 3.4% (they were described as 'non-intoxicating'). It followed the Cullen-Harrison Act, which was signed by President Franklin D. Roosevelt. As he put down the pen, he famously announced, 'I think this would be a good time to go for a beer.' Prohibition was fully repealed nine months later.

United Kingdom

National Beer Day is celebrated on 15 June. Beer Day Britain was instigated in 2015 by Jane Peyton, award-winning beer sommelier and founder of the School of Booze. The event is supported in kind by major organizations, including the Society of Independent Brewers and Associates, the British Beer and Pub Association (BBPA) and the Campaign for Real Ale and the Campaign for Real Ale (CAMRA).

Iceland

This is another country which annually celebrates the drink. On the first day of March, Icelanders raise a glass to the end of their Prohibition, which happened in 1989. It had begun seventy-four years earlier!

Rather than pour the beer into your mouth, why not apply the beer around it? Some swear by the beer face mask. Others – who don't like the smell – swear *about* it.

- 3 tbsp beer
- 1 tsp lemon or lime juice
- 1 egg white
- 1 small pinch ginger powder

 Pour the beer into a cereal bowl. Add the citrus juice, egg white and ginger. Whisk with a fork until nice and frothy.

 Put a towel around your shoulders to cover your chest. Apply the mask mix with cotton wool. Leave for 10 minutes before rinsing off.

Recipe

WELSH RAREBIT AKA GRILLED CHEESE

Also known as Welsh Rabbit, it originated in the 1700s – and no, rabbit is not one of the ingredients.

Bubbling, golden and hugely comforting, it's a rich, posh version of grilled cheese on toast.

A splash of beer is a welcome addition to the mix: a rich stout or ale, but not lager. If you like, scatter the grilled rarebit with finely chopped herbs such as chives or parsley. Or add a tablespoon of inexpensive chopped salted anchovy fillets to the mixture.

 **Serves 2**

- 2 big, thick slices of white bread
- 200g/7 oz Cheddar cheese, grated
- 2 tbsp beer
- 1 tsp Worcestershire sauce
- 2 tsp English mustard
- 1 small white onion, finely diced
- 1 medium-sized egg
- ground black pepper, to your taste

 In a large bowl, mix the grated cheese with the beer, Worcestershire sauce, mustard and diced onion to form a paste. Beat the egg with a fork and stir it into the mixture. Season with black pepper.

 Place the slices of bread on a baking tray and, under a low-medium grill, toast them on one side until golden.

 Turn the slices and spread the rarebit mixture onto the untoasted side. Return to the grill to cook until the cheese is nicely browned, runny and bubbling. Serve hot.

Do what it says on the tin (and the bottle). Recycle.

According to the recycling agency, Recycle More, every year around 9.591 billion drinks cans are produced in the United Kingdom, 75 per cent of which are recycled (about 7 billion). In the United States, 5.4 million cans are produced every hour. In 2023, 58 billion cans were recycled. That's a recycling rate of 43 per cent.

Perhaps the strangest episode of recycling took place at the Roskilde music festival in Denmark in 2015. The urine of festival-goers was collected in special metal troughs so that it could be used to make beer for fertilizing barley fields. This 'beer-cyling' also led to a Roskilde beer which is super eco-friendly, brewed by the Danish microbrewery Nørrebro Bryghus. This super eco-friendly beer is called – you guessed it – 'Pisner'.

Staying in Denmark ... Carlsberg Special Brew (not to everyone's taste) was first brewed in 1950 to commemorate Winston Churchill's visit to Copenhagen. Master brewers added notes of cognac to this strong lager as a nod to the British Prime Minister's drink of choice.

Recipe

IPA HOT SAUCE

Serve with grilled and pan-fried meats, roast chicken or cheeses — just about anything that needs a kick of spice.

 Makes 1 medium-sized jar

- 2 tbsp extra virgin olive oil
- 1 tsp smoked paprika
- 2 pinches sea-salt flakes
- 2 thyme sprigs, leaves picked
- 6 jalapeño peppers, coarsely chopped

- 1 medium onion, finely diced
- 6 garlic cloves, peeled and finely sliced
- 1 tbsp muscovado/dark brown sugar
- 350ml/12 fl oz IPA
- 2 tbsp white wine vinegar

 In a saucepan and over a low-medium heat, warm the olive oil and then add the paprika, thyme leaves and salt, along with the chopped jalapeños and diced onion. Gently sweat them in the pan for 5–7 minutes to soften the onion and jalapeños, but stir to prevent them browning.

 Add the garlic, sugar and vinegar and cook – still gently – for about 2 minutes. Now increase the heat to medium-high and pour in the beer, little by little. Bring to the boil and then reduce to a simmer and continue to simmer gently for 5–7 minutes, so that the beer reduces and thickens.

 Remove the pan from the heat and leave the hot sauce to cool down. Once cooled, blend to a purée. It's ready to enjoy. Transfer to jars and keep in the fridge.

~~~ *Hangover Cure* ~~~
MICHELADA
(MEXICAN BLOODY MARY)

Coconut water – drunk through a straw placed directly in the top of the coconut – has dealt with a zillion hangovers in the rum-loving Caribbean.

However, a beery hair of the dog is a Mexican Bloody Mary, also known as a Michelada. The vodka of the traditional Bloody Mary is replaced by beer – Corona and Modelo work well.

In Mexico, the rim of the glass is 'dressed' in salt or a chilli-salt mix (see Beer Salt, page 118). In goes the tomato juice, followed by the beer, and a strong squeeze of lime. Some like to half fill the glass with tomato juice and top up with beer and then continue to top up with the beer while drinking. The ratio of juice to beer is up to you, the drinker. Here's a version that's closer to the traditional Bloody Mary:

 Serves 1

- chilled tomato juice
- Worcestershire sauce
- Tabasco sauce (or your preferred chilli sauce)
- black pepper
- celery salt
- 1 lime, quartered
- 1 chilled bottle of beer

 Pour the tomato juice into a highball glass up to two-thirds full. Add the Worcestershire sauce, Tabasco, a few turns of the peppermill and a pinch of celery salt. Stir. Place a lime segment on the rim of the glass.

Recipe

CHOCOLATE, ORANGE AND WALNUT STOUT CAKE

A gorgeous cake celebrating the warmth of Guinness, although it can be replaced by chocolate stout or another stout of your choice.

 Serves 12

- 225g/8 oz/1 cup unsalted butter cubed, plus extra to grease the cake tin
- 250ml/8½ fl oz Guinness
- 100g/3½ oz cocoa powder
- 225g/8 oz muscovado/dark brown sugar

- 225g/8 oz eggs (about 4 medium eggs)
- 150ml/5 fl oz sour cream
- 225g/8 oz plain/all-purpose flour
- 2½ tsp bicarbonate of soda/baking soda

For the topping:

- 225g/8 oz full fat soft cheese
- 1 orange, zest only
- 100g/3 ½ oz/½ cup icing/powdered sugar
- 150ml/5 fl oz double/heavy cream
- 2–3 tbsp walnuts, chopped

Preheat the oven to 180°C/360°F. Butter and line the base of a 23cm (9 in) springform cake tin.

In a saucepan, bring the Guinness to the boil, then reduce the heat and simmer for 7 minutes. Add the cubed butter and continue to cook over a gentle heat until it has melted. Remove the pan from the heat and leave to cool.

In a large bowl, mix the cocoa powder, sugar and sifted flour. In a separate bowl, whisk the eggs and sour cream. Combine the flour mix with the eggs and sour cream, little by little. Pour in the

Guinness mixture, again little by little. Now stir in the bicarbonate of soda/bakings soda and combine well.

Pour the cake batter into the tin. Bake for about 60 minutes. Test it's done by inserting a skewer into the middle of the cake – if it comes out clean, the cake is cooked. (If not, put back in the oven and check again after 10 minutes.) Leave to cool in the tin.

To make the topping, beat the cheese until soft, then beat in the icing/powdered sugar a little at a time, and finally add the orange zest.

In a separate bowl, whisk the cream to soft peaks. Combine the whipped cream with the creamed cheese mixture, a little at a time.

Use a spatula to spread the icing over the cake. If you wish, smooth with a palette knife. Finally, decorate with the chopped walnuts and serve. The cake can be stored in the fridge for 5 days.

Forget Brasso, reach for a bottle instead. The acidity and carbonation of beer make it an ideal cleaning agent. It brings back the shine to metals such as gold, silver, brass and copper.

Soak a cloth in beer, wring it out and then rub your kitchen pans and photograph frames. Use it to polish your tankard, too. And be kind: offer to clean the tankards of family, friends and drinking mates. Rust can be removed from tools by submerging them overnight in beer.

Flat beer can also be used to deodorize shoes. Brush it onto the inner soles of the shoes, and you will find – toes crossed – that the natural yeast combats the foot smell.

36 BREW YOUR OWN

Are you an amateur or an anorak?

Over the years home brew kits have developed, and nowadays they are simple and quite effective to use.

Pinter, for instance, makes prepared branded packs for companies such as Guinness, BrewDog and many others. All that is required is to buy and add the necessary ingredients as a premix, and combine these with water and finish off the fermentation in the one self-contained unit, removing some of the solids from yeast stacks. The beer produces its own carbonation in the unit. It's like one of those food boxes delivered to cook at home – everything is prepared and all you have to do is cook.

Boil it, cool it and add the yeast, let it ferment and then package it. Wait – the number of days depends on the style of the beer – and it is ready to pour and drink.

Obviously, as the home brewer, you are subject to the recipe of the kit. Serious home brewers go back to the raw materials like obsessive chefs. They have their own boilers, pumps, aerators, chillers and fermenters, and they agonize over the quality of ingredients and the perfection of components. They are driven, perhaps, by a passion to brew for the sake of brewing, rather than for the sake of drinking inexpensive beer.

For more about home brewing, check out sites such as Grainfather and the American Homebrewers Association. Or proudly compete in a home-brew competition.

Recipe

BEEF BRISKET IN GUINNESS AND PRUNE JUICE

Many thanks to Marco Pierre White, the kitchen legend, who showed me how to make this hearty, wholesome casserole.

It was a cold, rainy day in London, and this dish turned out to be deeply comforting. 'As an extra garnish,' he said, 'you could sauté prunes and bacon lardons and spoon them over the beef at the end.'

 **Serves 4**

- 2 onions, quartered
- 6 garlic cloves, peeled
- extra virgin olive oil
- 500ml/17 fl oz prune juice
- 1 can of Guinness (550ml/ 19 fl oz)
- 200ml/7 fl oz good quality beef stock
- 1.4kg/3 lb beef brisket, trimmed and cut into 8 pieces

 First, preheat the oven to 150°C/300°F.

 Next, blend the onions and garlic in a food processor (or use a hand-held stick blender) to almost a purée.

 Heat 2–3 tablespoons of olive oil in a casserole dish, add the onion-garlic pulp and sweat over a low heat for a few minutes. Stir frequently, until the purée melts – but don't let it brown.

Remove the casserole from the heat and pour in the Guinness, prune juice and stock. Set aside.

 In a large heavy-based sauté pan, and over a medium heat, heat some olive oil – be generous with it – and then brown the beef for a minute or two on each side, turning only once. You might need to do this in batches – never overcrowd the pan. Remove the beef pieces and pat them dry with kitchen paper.

 Add the beef pieces to the casserole and transfer it to the oven to slowly cook for about 4 hours, or until the meat is delicately tender.

Make a wall clock to celebrate your preferred brews. You will need a clock mechanism, as well as a firm, square sheet of cardboard or plywood and scissors, glue, paints or pens, plus a dozen bottle caps from your best-loved bottled beers.

Draw a circle on the board – this will be the clock face. Cut it out with the scissors, or saw around the circle if using plywood. Put a hole in the middle – this is to fit the clock mechanism.

Paint or draw in the circle; be creative. Glue on the bottle cap, each cap representing a number on the clock, from one to twelve.

Fit the clock mechanism and the clock's hands. And after all that, it is definitely time for a beer.

Option: Use the round lid from a cake tin.

39

THE BEER BOTTLE
GARDEN GAME
(WITH LOTS OF NAMES)

Ever played Polish Horseshoes? You may know it by another name, as it is also called Beersbee, Bottle Bash, French Darts, Frisknock and (in Iceland) Fris-nok.

Players compete with a Frisbee to knock over a beer bottle that is sitting on top of the opponent's post or pole.

Create two teams and agree on a final score, which is typically 15 or 21 points. Place two poles about 40 feet apart and stand an empty beer bottle (or beer can) on top of one pole. In windy weather, fill the bottle with water or sand to stop it blowing away faster than the Frisbee. Toss a coin to decide which team goes first.

One team takes turns to throw the Frisbee to try to knock the bottle from the pole. The players in the other team try to catch the Frisbee before it hits the target. The player must throw with the Frisbee in one hand while holding a beer bottle in the other (as it's thirsty work).

When the opposing player catches the Frisbee, it's their turn to throw. Points are scored if a falling bottle is caught mid-air, and the winners must finish two points ahead.

40 MOVIE DRINKING GAMES

Barbie: Think pink! Sip every other time you see Barbie's Dreamhouse, and every other time you see a pink dress.

The Hangover: Drink every time you feel anxious for the characters.

Withnail and I: Drink every time the two main characters drink. Steady now.

Meet the Parents: Drink every time Mr Jinx, the cat, is mentioned.

The Godfather (I, II and III): Drink every time the word 'family' is mentioned (also works for the *The Fast and the Furious* franchise).

The Big Lebowski: Drink every time Jeffrey 'the Dude' Lebowski says 'dude'.

Jaws: Drink when you feel scared. Sip when someone jumps with fright. Drink when you hear *dun-dun, dun-dun, dun-dun …*

Use a roulette wheel and have a variety of beers to taste. Assign the numbers to different beers.

A roulette wheel has 37 slots – with one zero. A roulette wheel in the United States usually has 38 slots – with one zero, plus another slot for 00.

You might not have 37 or 38 different types of beer, but simply divide the numbers between the beers. So, for instance, one beer might have to be numbered 3, 12, 24 and 36.

Players are blindfolded, and spin the wheel. Another player passes them the beer which corresponds with the number. Points are scored when the beer is correctly identified.

Or ... if you don't have a roulette wheel, write numbers on paper and place them in a circle on a table. Place an empty bottle in the middle of the circle. A player spins the bottle to see which number it lands on. Drink the beer that matches the number and identify it correctly to win points.

'ALWAYS DO SOBER WHAT YOU SAID YOU'D DO DRUNK. THAT WILL TEACH YOU TO KEEP YOUR MOUTH SHUT.'

ERNEST HEMINGWAY

Cocktail

BLACK VELVET

'Grape or grain,' goes the saying, 'but never the twain.'

Of course there are exceptions to the rule of never mixing wine with beer, and few more satisfying than Black Velvet.

Made with equal amounts of Guinness (or stout) and champagne, it seems to meet the three 's' criteria for cocktails: sweet (the Guinness), sour (the acidity of the wine), strong (definitely).

Often it is served in a champagne flute. However, Harry Craddock, the legendary barman at the Savoy Hotel in the

1920s and '30s, served it in a 'tall tumbler'. Meanwhile, in Ian Fleming's *Diamonds Are Forever*, we learn that James Bond prefers a sizeable version of the drink. He offers to take Bill Tanner, MI6 Chief of Staff, for 'dressed crab and a pint of Black Velvet' at Scott's, the seafood restaurant in Mayfair.

When you serve, why not entertain your guests with the charming story of Black Velvet's creation? This cocktail originated in 1861 at Brooks's, the gentlemen's club in St James's Street, London, at a time when the nation was in mourning following the death of Queen Victoria's husband, Prince Albert. In a eureka moment, the club's bartender reached for the black stuff, announcing something like: 'Champagne, too, shall be in mourning.'

 **Serves 1**

- half Guinness (or your preferred stout, chilled)
- half champagne (or another sparkling wine, chilled)

 Pour the Guinness into a champagne glass, leaving space for the champagne. Place an upturned spoon over the Guinness. Now carefully pour the champagne over the spoon so that it almost floats on top of the Guinness.

 Do not stir and certainly do not shake – this is not a Bond Martini!

43

HOW GREEN IS YOUR GARDEN?

The yeast and sugars in beer can help speed up the decomposition of organic matter in a compost pile, making it a useful addition to your compost bin.

Beer is also rich in nitrogen, which breaks down the micro-organisms, while the sugars feed those micro-organisms. The liquid itself provides moisture to the compost, enabling the bacteria to thrive. Less is more, however. Don't soak the compost in beer, but add it in moderation. Turn the compost from time to time to aid aeration. Use flat beer.

Flat beer – with no artificial additives – can also be used as a fertilizer. It is rich in magnesium, phosphorous and potassium, all of which are beneficial to plant growth and health. The yeast in beer acts as food for soil microbes.

Mix one-part flat beer to ten parts cold water, and pour onto the soil around the base of plants, or directly onto grass.

Recipe

BEER BLINIS

Little buckwheat pancakes, blinis are best served straight from the pan, topped with smoked salmon and crème fraîche, or grated cheese such as Gruyère.

 Makes at least 12 blinis

- 60g/2½ oz strong plain/bread flour
- 60g/2½ oz buckwheat flour
- 6g/¼ oz fresh yeast (or use the equivalent of dry yeast)
- 75ml/2½ fl oz whole milk
- 1½ tbsp sour cream
- 2 medium eggs, separated
- 50ml/2 fl oz dark beer

- ½ tsp salt
- unsalted butter, for frying

 In a large bowl, combine the flour and salt. In a saucepan on a low heat, gently warm the milk to body temperature. Whisk in the yeast. Mix the egg yolks with the sour cream and combine with the warm milk-yeast mixture. Stir this mixture into the flour. Pour in the beer, add the salt, and whisk to create a thick batter. Cover with a kitchen towel and leave in a warm part of the kitchen for at least 1½ hours.

 Lightly whisk the egg whites and gently fold them into the batter. Cover again and leave them for 1½ hours.

When it's time to cook the blinis, heat some of the butter in a crêpe pan (or frying pan/skillet). For each blini, use a tablespoon of batter. Cook on a low-medium heat, until the underside is golden. Flip, and do the other side. The edges should be crispy. The heat is too high if bubbles appear on the top of the blini, so remove the pan from the heat for a few seconds.

It's a long-running debate among beer lovers: does Guinness actually taste better in Ireland?

The answer is yes. But find out for yourself by heading to the source – the Guinness Storehouse in Dublin – to taste the dark stuff fresh from the tap.

Located at St. James's Gate, the Storehouse is the site of Arthur Guinness, the original brewery. Today it's a full-blown experience set over seven floors that dives into the history, brewing process and cultural impact of the world's most famous stout. In the tour, you'll see the original 9,000-year lease Arthur Guinness signed in 1759 and learn about the magic of this brew.

Hungry, too? The Storehouse not only has bars but also restaurants where you can pair your pint with Irish classics like beef stew or Guinness-infused desserts. But the best part? You can drink your own face. Well, sort of. Using Ripples technology, your selfie can be printed onto the creamy head of a pint. Known as a 'Stoutie', it is made with a natural malt extract, so it's completely safe (and delicious) to drink. Top it all off with a visit to the Gravity Bar, where you'll enjoy a complimentary pint and panoramic views of Dublin.

Recipe

BEER SYRUP

The beer-lover's replacement for maple syrup or golden syrup.

Drizzle over pancakes, sponge cake, porridge, granola, bacon and, of course, cocktails, ice cream (see Guinness and Brown-Bread Ice Cream, page 13) and ice cream floats (see Chocolate Stout and Ice Cream Float, page 122). Spice it up by adding freshly chopped chilli pepper to the pan before making the syrup.

Makes 1 medium jar

- 400ml/14 fl oz flat beer (stout is ideal)
- 200g/1 cup caster/baker's sugar
- 100g/½ cup muscovado/dark brown sugar
- 1 large orange, juiced
- 1 tbsp liquid honey

 Combine the beer, sugars and half of the orange juice in a large, deep sauté pan or large saucepan. Bring to the boil over a medium heat and then reduce to low-medium to simmer gently until it reduces to a light syrup. This will take about 15 minutes.

 Remove the pan from the heat, add the honey and the rest of the orange juice, and swirl the pan a little. Leave to cool for 5 minutes.

 Gently stir the cooled syrup, and while still hot transfer it to a clean bottle – a clean beer bottle, perhaps – or a jar. Seal with a lid (or cap if using a beer bottle) and keep in the fridge.

Before you begin, please check out the beer painting by the Oklahoma-born artist Karen Eland. She's at karenelandart.com.

Once you have seen her beer masterpieces, you will feel deeply inspired by what can be accomplished and want to try it yourself. She also paints with coffee.

Karen says that watercolor paper is key, as beer can't soak into a canvas. She uses the Arches brand.

Simply pour stout or porter into a bowl and start there. Though Karen recommends microwaving the beer for about a minute at a time to condense it to an even darker and thicker 'paint'.

It's best to work light to dark. You will build up several layers to get the darkest areas, and you can add water to do the lighter areas.

Unlike watercolors, the beer will come back off the

paper to some degree. Correct a mistake by adding a small amount of water with a clean brush onto the area you want to remove. Blot immediately with a clean paper towel and the spot will be much lighter. Or, says Karen, intentionally use this technique to create interesting light-on-dark effects.

Once the painting is thoroughly dry, spray it with a UV-varnish such as Krylon UV Resistant Clear. Frame it with a mat or spacers so that it doesn't directly touch the glass.

'BEER IS PROOF
THAT GOD
LOVES US AND
WANTS US TO
BE HAPPY.'

BENJAMIN FRANKLIN

48 BEER SALT

A quirky trick that can transform a beer. The salt not only adds its own taste but enhances the taste of a brew.

It originated in Latin America and was introduced to Texas by Mexicans. The Mexicans know it as *chelada*: the rim of the glass (or bottle) is salted and served with a lime segment. Squeeze the lime into the beer, or bite into the fruit. Drink. Traditionalists insist that a *chelada* must also have ice in the glass. If in Texas, ask for your beer to be 'dressed' and it will (should) come with a salted rim. It has since become big business (Twang, the San Antonio-based company, produces unique-tasting salts).

Make different beer salts at home by adding lime zest or dried chilli to the salt. Some Texans simply add a pinch to the liquid in the glass or bottle. As for the beer to drink with salt, try a chilled Modelo Especial, the pilsner-styled lager from Mexico that is crisp, dry and refreshing. Enjoy with tacos. See also the Michelada Hangover Cure, page 81.

You've drunk your beer – now why not wear it? Transform beer bottle caps into eye-catching earrings.

Whether they are vintage caps from your preferred brew, or from a bottle popped on a special occasion, these make unusual and meaningful accessories. Bonus: it's eco-friendly. Bottle caps are among the top ten most common litter items found on beaches and in waterways. So why not turn waste into wearable art?

You will need: two metal beer bottle caps; pliers; a hammer; sandpaper; earring hooks; a nail.

Collect and clean your beer bottle caps. Flatten the caps using pliers and a hammer. (You can remove the white rubbery insert from the inside if you prefer.)

Sand down any sharp edges. Mark where you'll make a hole at the top, then use a small nail and hammer to create that hole.

Attach the earring hooks. Enjoy your unique and upcycled beer-rings.

The combination of beer and ice cream might not appeal to all tastes, but choose the right beer to go with the right ice cream, and on a summer's day it can become an instant crowd-pleaser.

Avoid beers which are too bitter or overly hoppy. Stouts (such as Guinness, Murphy's, Beamish) are fine, but the best choice is a chocolate stout. This is typically creamy and usually brewed with cacao nibs and chocolate malt. Think notes of bitter chocolate, coffee and vanilla.

As for the types of ice cream: vanilla, chocolate and coffee work well. Use a tall glass, such as a highball or a pint glass.

To make two beer floats: simply place a scoop or two of ice cream – chocolate, vanilla or coffee – in each glass. Pour over the chilled stout and drizzle with beer syrup (see page 112).

Once you've made your Chocolate Stout and Ice Cream Float, why not drink it while lying on a floating pool mattress? And consider the history of the floating brewery ...

During World War II, the British dispatched HMS *Menestheus* to troops in the Pacific Theatre. The steam-powered vessel contained a 55-barrel brewery system. Its mission: to supply troops with beer. Mission accomplished. Every week, about 250 barrels of Davy Jones mild ale were produced on board.

What an amazing morale booze-ter!

Recipe

BEER GRANITA

Stop! Do NOT tip away those beer dregs from last night. Flat beer is the perfect ingredient for beer granita, an Italian-style semi-slushie made with crushed ice.

If you have more flat beer than you know what to do with, adapt this recipe using an approximate ratio of 1:5 sugar to beer. So, about one cup of sugar to every five cups of beer. Pilsner works well here.

 Serves 4–6

- 100g/½ cup caster/baker's sugar
- 100ml/½ cup water
- 1 orange, juice only
- 480ml/2 cups flat beer
- 2 pinches ground ginger

 In a saucepan and over a low heat, gently heat the sugar, water, orange juice and ginger until the sugar has dissolved – though don't bring it to a boil.

 Pour in the beer. Now transfer the granita mix to a shallow baking tray or container and place in the freezer. After 90 minutes, scrape the top with a fork and return it to the freezer. Repeat this scraping process four more times, every hour.

 Serve in glasses, drizzled with beer syrup (see recipe, page 112).

ABOUT THE AUTHOR

James Steen is an award-winning journalist, author, ghostwriter and editor. He has collaborated with legendary chefs and celebrities, as well as business people, restaurateurs, hoteliers, a rock star and an intensive care nurse. He co-authored the autobiographies of Marco Pierre White, Raymond Blanc, Keith Floyd and Ken Hom. He has co-written many cookbooks, including *White Heat 25*, *The Ritz London: The Cookbook* and *Le Manoir aux Quat'Saisons: The Story of a Modern Classic*. Steen's other books include *The World of All Creatures Great and Small*, *The Kitchen Magpie* and *50 Greatest Dishes of the World*.

ACKNOWLEDGEMENTS

I am raising my glass – and owe a large drink – to those who assisted in the creation of this strange little book. They include: Nell Warner, my wise (and patient) editor at Michael O'Mara; designers Natasha Le Coultre and Claire Cater; Alice Fewery, copy editor; Vicky Bywater, proofreader; Derek Prentice M.B.E., renowned Master Brewer and co-founder of Wimbledon Brewery; Marco ('I'm just a cook') Pierre White. Daisy Steen, thank you for helping with research – I'll make you a beautiful pair of glittering beer-rings.

- 100g/½ cup caster/ baker's sugar
- 100ml/½ cup water
- 1 orange, juice only
- 480ml/2 cups flat beer
- 2 pinches ground ginger

 In a saucepan and over a low heat, gently heat the sugar, water, orange juice and ginger until the sugar has dissolved – though don't bring it to a boil.

 Pour in the beer. Now transfer the granita mix to a shallow baking tray or container and place in the freezer. After 90 minutes, scrape the top with a fork and return it to the freezer. Repeat this scraping process four more times, every hour.

 Serve in glasses, drizzled with beer syrup (see recipe, page 112).

ABOUT THE AUTHOR

James Steen is an award-winning journalist, author, ghostwriter and editor. He has collaborated with legendary chefs and celebrities, as well as business people, restaurateurs, hoteliers, a rock star and an intensive care nurse. He co-authored the autobiographies of Marco Pierre White, Raymond Blanc, Keith Floyd and Ken Hom. He has co-written many cookbooks, including *White Heat 25*, *The Ritz London: The Cookbook* and *Le Manoir aux Quat'Saisons: The Story of a Modern Classic*. Steen's other books include *The World of All Creatures Great and Small*, *The Kitchen Magpie* and *50 Greatest Dishes of the World*.

ACKNOWLEDGEMENTS

I am raising my glass – and owe a large drink – to those who assisted in the creation of this strange little book. They include: Nell Warner, my wise (and patient) editor at Michael O'Mara; designers Natasha Le Coultre and Claire Cater; Alice Fewery, copy editor; Vicky Bywater, proofreader; Derek Prentice M.B.E., renowned Master Brewer and co-founder of Wimbledon Brewery; Marco ('I'm just a cook') Pierre White. Daisy Steen, thank you for helping with research – I'll make you a beautiful pair of glittering beer-rings.